THE FORESTS OF AUTUMN

Poems

THE FORESTS OF AUTUMN

Poems

Ken Fontenot

ALAMO BAY PRESS
SEADRIFT•AUSTIN

Copyright © 2025 by Ken Fontenot

All rights reserved. No part of this book may be reproduced in any form without permission in writing from the publisher, except by a reviewer who may quote brief passages in a review.

Cover Art: Octavio Quintanilla
Book Design by ABP

Alamo Bay Press

Lowell Mick White, Editor
Diane Wilson, Activist

Pamela Booton, Director
825 W 11th St Ste 114
Austin, Texas 78701
pam@alamobaypress.com
www.alamobaypress.com

ISBN 978-1-943306-28-2
Library of Congress Control Number: 2024945498

For my New Orleans family with affection and gratitude

and

For my friend Tom who gifted me the book's title

with

Thanks to Peter Cooley and Rodney Jones for their help in our critique sessions

Part One
Hospital, 2020

& Nouns	3
A Far Better Painter Than I	4
A Tree's Shade	6
Address to the Self	7
After Ida, Now That We Have Power Again	8
An Arsenic Crab	9
Asking	10
Close Call	11
Dachshunds	12
East New Orleans	13
Ending With the First-Person Plural	14
Entering the Broom's Straw	15
Feral Cat	16
Forgotten	17
Four Stanzas	18
Glory Be	19
He Farmed in Evangeline Parish	20
Here's a Day's Worth	21
Homage to Ashbery	22
Hospital, 2020	23

Part Two
Simply Pinholes

"I lived in the first century of world wars."	27
If Only, a Persona Poem	29
Invocation of Angels, a Persona Poem	30
Jackie Eliot, 1985	31

Johnson Escalates a War	32
Language: French, Latin, German	33
Lunar	34
Me and One I Imagine	35
Missing My German	36
Money, Gratis	37
My Friend and I	38
Naming and Other Entrances	39
New Day	40
Not Just a Thought	41
O Friend	42
Once at a Zoo in England	43
Professor	44
Quotidian	45
Rebuttal	46
Seed Time	47
Simply Pinholes	48

Part Three
The Forests of Autumn

Sisters	51
Sixties Blues	52
Special Place	54
Spring 2	55
T'ang Inspiration	56
Teachers On the Beach	57
Text Message to the Gods	58
The Congress Avenue Bridge	59
The Earth, Running Out of Time	60

The Few That Get Away	61
The German Word for "Cook"	62
The Homelessness of Fish	63
The Questions	64
This Early	65
Time to Come Inside	66
Tiny Comet	67
To Have a Sense for Animals	68
The Forests of Autumn	69
Werner Drive	70
What I Still Feel	71
What Money Is Like	72
What Spirit	73
What Was I Thinking?	74
With Dancing in Mind	75
Years Before His Insanity	76
Acknowledgements	79
About Ken Fontenot	81
About Octavio Quintanilla	83

Part One
Hospital, 2020

& Nouns

The simpler the equation, the happier the student
mathematician, his love akin to his favorite dessert.

> That was my humble experience once, anyway.

I like to forgo bodybuilding and rudeness.
I like to be me often rather than sometimes. A polymath
I'm not. So let the clouds wander everywhere they wish.
Let people enjoying their meals have at it. What?

> The dog has gotten under the fence again tonight?

It's a night when one can see both Venus and Mars,
a night relatives gather to celebrate a common ancestry.
Stars wink at me. I'm touched! Thanks for your attention
in a nation happy only when the stock market peaks.

Already the moon going from incomplete to complete.
Already time keeps running around like a racehorse.
Time and gravity. Both things we just see the results of.

> Everyone sees a hospital as a parking garage for
> pain.

Sleeping? I slept through adjectives. Everywhere. & nouns.

A Far Better Painter Than I

Brecht, born in the same year as my grandfather.
The former a writer, the latter a farmer who went
only to the fourth grade. Their lives so different,
I feel an attraction to both. So. Both wise.
Both able to live single-mindedly. And firm.
Their smoking—who knew then?—led to heart attacks.

I have always loved those who let nothing distract
them. Do such people have a full life behind them?
Just as I have always loved flowers for their
steady growth. Roses still demand our attention.
They still take effect when attached to a dancer's hair.

Cultivate American Beauty roses! Pay attention to lilies!
O my student named Rose. I will commit myself
to teaching her German with her great feel for language.
So sad to hear that her cousin's boyfriend took her life.
One wonders how these things begin. One wonders
at which point it didn't have to happen. The hapless girl
realized the worst and tried to escape. Obsessions
in feelings! A soul unable to love or feel pleasure!

I speak as someone who has seen what most never see.
A former inmate in a psychiatric ward, I lived with
cases touch and go before my eyes. Those in danger
to themselves and others. Thieves. Outcasts. Junkies.
Alcoholics with delirium tremens. Repeat offenders. People
who believed they were kings and presidents and rock stars.

Being bilingual, having traveled, having lived
in a co-op residence with many different sorts of people,
having grown up in a home where a lot went wrong,
I feel as if I exist with a crown full of stars.
I call this the starry effect—much shines in my eyes.
Let me ask, therefore, that whoever is born later
take an interest in my work, my silent work, in an age
where so many poets need to ply their pens.
Where poets have friends who can get them other friends.
Unlike Apollinaire, I don't ask you to take pity on me.
And still there is the sun. A far better painter than I.

A Tree's Shade

It is beautiful to have made my way
past the breaking point without breaking,
and instead to have smelled the flowers.
In the palace of stars have I lived.
In the moonlight have I made my wishes.
I took the liberty to keep moving like the blood.
I took a chance at being a poet with no certainty.
Poems I don't even remember have been set down.
For those who want to know what it was like
to live in an age where change was the rule.
And where it required a malleable mind to survive.
It is beautiful to stay in the tree's shade
on a hot day, and I am still at it.

Address to the Self

Forget fame, Fontenot. Legion are those who
need to push their way to the front of the line.
Find the stars enchanting. And not even our souls
have had to hurry in order to get here. Be content.
As long as musicians give us something to dance to.
The sea shines. The wind listens. The moon bathes.

After Ida, Now That We Have Power Again

Life and history are akin to our dissatisfaction
with the way our living rooms are arranged.
It won't do. Something must be changed. Now.
We would even be willing to fight for such change.
Is the world better? Maybe not. Just different.

I, too, am this "we". Everyone is. But the self: not life.
Since without anything else, it's a beggar, a castaway,
shipwrecked. For us the moon is only another light
amidst a world of lights. But the moon must teach wonder.
As the whale should, with its great sea-mastery.

Today I saw a huge tree, all its roots exposed,
the sidewalk broken, the storm gone like a criminal.
Its trunk fell across the road, blocking traffic.
Soon I heard the whining: necessary chainsaws.
Not far away, in Terrebonne Parish, people are
hungry but receive food from those more fortunate,
those who survived the hurricane relatively intact.
I'd like to think there would be some lesson here.
All I know to say: let's brace ourselves for the next one.

Ken Fontenot

An Arsenic Crab

A poem can break my heart in a most cerebral way.
Who can say why or how? But I can say: wow.
Enough to make me want to write what is loved, sweet
as a face. As those who train dogs with their spirit.
And there has to be some solid images building up.
There has to be great grit, great grace as well.
I'm even tempted to take out my Billy Collins to read.
I'm even tempted to start such a poem as a story.

So. Dylan Thomas said "once below a time." I think it
best to keep to tradition. Once upon a time, in spring,
birds' eyes returned from bitter cold in winter.
Nests became pouches for the soon-to-be-born.
Clouds were more admired than sitcoms, than Nixon.
I built a tree house, home to an entire neighborhood
of kids. We smoked there without our parents knowing.
I was king of us animals from the deep jungles.
We shot arrows at targets. Once a boy brought a knife.
Inadvertently and close to the heart, he stabbed a friend
who survived. Mothers worried. But fathers still went
to work. The past finally took out life insurance.
The future could have gone up in smoke, an arsenic crab.

Asking

Kids ask me what the secret of things is. A difficult
question. I can only answer: I don't know. As I pat
Mystery on the back. Mystery: silent, thus innocent.
Innocent as a noiseless hummingbird doing its job.
The outdoors calls to me. Grass, trees, a lake,
a fishing boat are all I need. They complete the rest
of the landscape, as important as a mountain.

The beings—beneath the rock I lift in the forest—
interest me. They have made a home almost like
the ants have with their dirt castle, their place to hide.
How quiet they go about living, how praiseworthy!
I'll honor them with a prayer. But I'll ask nothing
of Fate, not even a kindness, for it is already so busy.

Close Call

The walls of the coffee shop would seem empty as
a blue sky, without their artwork. But ekphrastic poems
are farthest from me, having become a fad.
The point: not to describe the paintings—
a lesser poet can do that—but to say
what the work is trying hard to mean to us.
Rilke saw this when he responded to an archaic statue
with his wisdom, "You must change your life."

I would like my poem to be as transparent as
the huge window I look through. As transparent
as what the cop's doing, not ticketing a motorist.

More often than not the sun is maternal, helps all.
Even the wind holds my attention. Strong as it is
today, making the row of plastic flags in a used car lot
stiffen, as it did to clothes once on Mom's clothesline.
In the fifties my mother made sure I was well dressed
for school. My first-grade class picture showed me
different from each of the other boys who wore long pants.
My short pants as well as my shirt, starched and pressed.
That photo vanished for good in the waters of Katrina.

The sun has set. I get in my car and drive down
Claiborne Avenue, headed soon to the expressway.
Suddenly I see a woman—faded dress, bone-thin, toothless—
as she tries to cross the street, not at the light.
She steps into my lane. I hit my brake and miss
striking her. Roll down my window. "Ma'am, are you
all right?" "Sorry, sir, but I'm—I'm nearly blind."
"Well, be careful out there." And my heart: still racing.

The Forests of Autumn

Dachshunds

These words equal not so much a creation as a discovery.
I locate the dachshunds in a place, but they are
Already there, for it's their mother who created them.
Not I. I think of the literal meaning of this name.
Badger dog. The similarity: in the stubby, short legs
With an elongated body. One wild, the other domesticated.

Martin and Lewis were my friend Kenny's favorite children.
Finally, off to dog heaven, they spoke with me before.
"Don't call us wienie dogs. It's politically incorrect."
I persisted. "What is it like, guys, to have all the love
One can ask for?" "We deserve it, as Wagner believed
He was so special he could evade his creditors."
"When I walked in earlier, both you guys barked at me.
Only my petting you helped to stop your grumbling."
Martin: "Not even humans are in a good mood all
The time. Learn to forgive your human grouches as well."

It was spring. I escorted the boys to the backyard.
What days these were, magical like the time of circuses
And cool like one always seems to be in dreams. Day moon
With a belly. Everything appeared to have just awakened.
Everything, especially the birdhouses, full of
Activity. I put seed in the bird feeder. Cardinals
Came and went. So did sparrows. The backyard,
Its own aviary. Flowers in bloom: Turk's Cap, Cenizo,
Morning Glory, American Beautyberry, Esperanza.
Two squirrels chased each other up and down the oak.

It was time to go inside. Just as we might be waked by name,
So too we call our animals, our anthropomorphic ones.

Ken Fontenot

East New Orleans

Dear Werner Drive, why have you swallowed all
of my boyhood friends, the diabetic James Lemoine
who didn't make it past forty, and Jimmy Rouquette
who wound up missing in Vietnam, part of
the universe's magical disappearance act few
return from. And Robert Mayo's father.
He chain-smoked Pall Malls until his heart finally
quit on his fifty-sixth birthday, Robert taking
a bullet near Saigon. The world seems more ghostly
without you. None of you can even dream me anymore.
But I am left to dream you. I am left to empoem you.
No one ever promised we'd be together in old age,
which has its own demands, when memory finds
it difficult to think of what one ate the morning before.
But I can still put down the best words in the best
order, to recall what Coleridge said. I can still lift
my eyes to the clouds, who've kept an eye on all of us.

Ending With the First-Person Plural

I ask you to select the correct answer. Is it
(a) because the moon has never wanted to be hugged
or (b) because the fish insist the ocean is theirs
or (c) because volcanoes keep agreeing to nothing
or (d) all of the above? Such things occur in existence,
not on some remote star I cannot even conjure up.
I am wounded by blood on your face since I don't
know your assailant. I give you my promise to keep
all promises. Is this logical? Do you think it will work?

Enliven yourself. Awaken. Be a silent negotiator.
One who observes everything: only rapt, astonished.
I have wondered how quickly now it will take you
to be a bright star, to be an open door, to be a gift.
We are always encircling horizons, always outlasting fear.

Entering the Broom's Straw

This summer on the coast we expect hurricanes.
More than ever. I will keep a dispassionate eye open.
I will try my best to praise my city's joie de vivre.

And the old monuments in my city have come down.
With the Tulsa race riots in mind, Tulsa burning,
I am to look to history not for the achievements
of the victors, but for the sufferings of the vanquished.
Historians tell all the truth but tell it slant, as
Dickinson would have it. Some things they neglect.
Others they exaggerate. A foggy day engulfs history.
To read a good book of poems seems more truthful.
But to earn their places, even poets must be judged.

I need to enter a broom's straw while I perceive
the mop's faith. Soon cleaning becomes part of me.
With broom and mop being the center of everything.
I revolve, today, around them as earth around the sun.

And here I knock at a crawfish mound to try
to see how they live in the ground. No answer.
More than to the point, I love to eat boiled crawfish.
The heavy artillery of their tails. A Cajun's paradise.

Feral Cat

Rain with its distant sound of furniture being dragged.
But it's hard to recall the voice I had before I matured
into a young man. And my voice addressing my sister
is different from my voice should it yell for help.
Different, too, from the one in an impression of John Wayne.

And so, this beautiful spring fades into a summer
where a devil of a hurricane has a chance to enter
the Gulf of Mexico and hence maybe my famous city.
This I know: someone along the coast will have to fret.
From the southmost point of Texas all the way to Florida.
Possible bull's-eyes. I think of the many years I endured
them and am grateful to the gods I survived. Whew!
Still, I see on the news always angry weather elsewhere
also. Yet, I have faith in young people and their plans.

(Hello, feral cat. We all have reasons for living. What's yours?)

Forgotten

Dawn was climbing on my back like a child.
Morning stretched far. Always the sun painting.
Always the day moon either complete or not.

Then inside, I thought: wow, so that's where they were!
My class rings: high school and college, in a cigar box
not opened for forty years. Friends of the hurting earth,
both unwearable, my fingers thick with weight I put on.

I was young. Headstrong. I argued with my father,
a gentle man. Now I wished I could take it all back.
Each of my dogs over the years—how unselfish they were.
How pure in their love. Something everyone should learn.
The mind knows these things. But has the heart forgotten?

Four Stanzas

The drawings at Lascaux remind me of the courage
to be original. And the joy. Even though lately originality
is a new mixture of influences. Mothers and fathers
having preceded me, and offspring, my contemporaries.

I think I got by so well in German because
my pronunciation was nearly perfect, unlike others
in their struggle with the variety of German sounds.
Why does the ear falter while imitating another language?
So I imitate other poets easily. Selecting certain things.
I make my own syntax, varied, rich in my idiolect.

What is the idiolect of painters? Who think in colors,
shapes, light. One thumbprint this artist, one, another.

In the painting I see now, there's hope and a hint of birds.
It will be the cover art for my latest book of poems.
The drawings at Lascaux remind us of courage.

Ken Fontenot

Glory Be

One keeps only a few great friends.
The others, tested, are still at a distance.
Though they do not deter me from the heavens.
Since even the moon can be a priest.
I, too, listen to confessions from the earth.
I welcome them the way someone who tends
a garden welcomes the weeds as much as the lilies.
"Long live the weeds." (Hopkins) He understood.
And his friend Bridges kept his poems alive.
Bridges sensed him as one apart,
an original without an ounce of tired thinking.
One of the many I go to for my own work.
Poems I hope another poet can take from,
in which case I would feel utterly honored.

For what else would I feel honored? To be
in the stars' silent presence. To watch
a hummingbird doing its silent task.
To find a certain day I wish for all days.

O glory be to the ocean's waves giving a lecture
on persistence. Glory be to the female
releasing her pups. Glory be to the air
the lungs give back, unselfishly, as a prayer.

He Farmed in Evangeline Parish

Summer's barn outlasted the summer, only to greet
It again after the passing of other seasons.
And as a kid I pointed to a calf my grandpa
Said was mine. His life itself: generous-spirited.
Upon his death I wailed the loudest of everyone
And could not be comforted. The funeral home
Stayed full. So many from his parish loved him.
Much of his Cajun French remained with me. Thus,
My high school standard French proved easy to master.
For in New Orleans my father, the farmer's son, found work.
But a Parisian neighbor said our French was bad French.
Because of that I always defended the black idiom
As meaningful. All languages attempt to unite.
Still, we praise those who transcend: the polyglots.

Here's a Day's Worth

The bees arrived and then the bees arrived.
I felt like their wings had stars in them.
But let's move from the past to the present
as if we were moving into a new house. Let's nap.

I am just about to present my bill to the Evil Spirit.
It still owes, and the world seems to know as much.
Yet I would be lying if I said that everything
is lovelier than ice cream. It simply isn't.
Although orange bicycles can be pleasant to ride.

The consonants appear to be as happy as vowels.
Today I have a mouthful of all of them,
diphthongs included. The sun lights my name that
I speak times when the heat enters my mouth like a gag.
But it's been a long day. So I'll open my book of dreams.

Homage to Ashbery

I don't wish I were someone else, but to have
His art savvy, his vision, would be nice. Sparrows,
For example, must be happy in their bird bodies.
They come and set themselves down like commas.

Yet, to talk or not to. Silence can be a bet that pays off.
(What do you know, friend of the earth now in trouble?)
My poet buddy Rette Maddox wrote that tragedy teaches:
No one ever learns anything. Is it overstatement?
Are there exceptions? What do we gather growing older?
I'd rather be no place but here. Content to keep scribbling.
Content to watch the metal glare, a tiny daylight star.
I've been reading Ashbery. Can't you tell, you lover
Of nonlinear thinking? Even I don't know where
I'm going with all of this. Ashbery puts us off.
He circles the wagons just for the sake of circling.
But he's credible. Usually. How long it has taken
For me to value him! How long the hawk must
Circle before it decides it's time—ah—to dive!

Ken Fontenot

Hospital, 2020

I was caught up in the last syllable
of my name which not everyone pronounced
correctly, pronouncing the final "t".
I like my last name. It comes from a man
born in Poitiers, France in the early part
of the eighteenth century. Stationed in the French
militia in Mobile, Alabama. Moved to Louisiana.
A true Frenchman among Cajuns from Nova Scotia.
No wonder I've always wanted to be a Frenchman!
Even in Paris my shadow would follow like a friend.

My shadow just beneath the skin is praiseworthy.
So is the idea of my mind feeling its way around.
But keep me out of the hospital where many have pulled
into parking spaces of suffering. Ah, if only family were
allowed to be close to the dying in their helplessness.
That would be ideal. That would comfort.
I have watched body bags being stored in cold trucks.
I have watched the sick turned over on their bellies.
Yet to recover is to regain the temporary use of oneself
until something else happens. O angels—in scrubs
and white coats, in danger yourselves, whose wings
are beating quickly for the time being—stay resolute.

Listen to the epidemiologists? Of course.
I can't call myself a lucky self without them.

Part Two
Simply Pinholes

"I lived in the first century of world wars."

—Muriel Rukeyser

I was so hungry, even a banana made sense.
From the cosmos came unanimous voices: hurrah!
I wonder if Apollinaire ever became an epicure.
Yes, I started reading him again. Poor guy!
A victim of World War I. If only he had lived.
His not the case with other artists in the nineteenth
and twentieth centuries, lives shortened by TB.
Had it been any other writer I would have asked:
what about those always in the throes of their moods?
But he was the real enchilada. A poet's king.
I have taken his surrealism gladly to heart.

Unlike with Apollinaire and his theorist Breton,
I don't think just one manifesto is possible today.
Too many different experiments current in poetry.
Even now I am caught up, for example, in Bly's
leaping poetry ideas of 1975. Translations
give us so many keyholes, so many models.
I still find Lorca amazing. And Neruda.
With his ideological stance. Brecht, too, his
sociopolitical concerns. He used Apollinaire's feelings
as grist in his poem "To Posterity". Both wanted
to be judged kindly for the times in which they lived.

German writers born during and after World War II
still feel shame for the Holocaust. But they
wish for their people not to bear their shame
as long as others bear their crimes. This shame
goes so deep that they no longer know
whether there were ever any human beings
at all who were allowed to live unmolested.

I walk into the afternoon. The wind caresses.
The sun's light is maternal. And helps everyone.

If Only, a Persona Poem

In memory of Nicolas Born

If only you could walk into that movie,
unnoticed, playing the character who is
really Mia Farrow, but it could be you.
If only you could walk into the front
of a book and leave by the back. Let me not
forget it is sweeter to love you than not to.
My feeling is that spring will welcome everyone.
Our dogs plan our lives, and not the other way
around. The sea says "shh" to children like
a teacher. Everywhere air enters the lungs
and leaves, a different air. Get all the oxygen
you can, long-distance runner, mountain climber
of my life. I too have need of exhaustion.
I too count on a brave and different day.

Invocation of Angels, a Persona Poem

We have given up our selves for another self.
Which is called marriage. Even the gods recognize it.
But sometimes the self gets so heavy
it escapes into a kingdom different from the world.
It's called the "not-me", which we visit
whenever the earth itself seems foreign.

Meanwhile we notice the animals don't complain
and wonder why we ourselves must do so.
Such mystery, such unpredictability
lies at the very center. Thus our clothes
become the small houses we live in.
And the sky, that blue we can't touch,
rescues us, on sunny, fortuitous days.

The trick: not to want to figure out why
many questions have no answers,
for "why" is the wrong question. (Love them all.)
After all, not even Whitman knew what makes
the grass grass. Here spirit enters as a belief.
We begin to treasure just naming things.
Many moons, in their wisdom, float by,
especially in the dreams of perceptive children.
O angels, look, a tree. In its silence it understands
that no one has a monopoly on grief,
that Saturday nights are a time for dancing.

Jackie Eliot, 1985

The murderer, too, was once a child in need of parents.
He learned to straighten his room, to eat over his plate
and spare his mother from cleaning his crumbs, and keep
from soiling the shirt she, in her love, would have to wash.

Years later, after rape and murder, the judge said, "You're
just a time bomb waiting to explode. I'm debating whether
to sentence you to death." He said, "Go for it, if you want!"
The judge grew livid, banging her gavel on the bench.
"Not only will I go for it, but I'll make sure you will
never kill again!" He was an adopted orphan from London.
His attorney tried to extradite him to where he was born.
During the sixties Great Britain abolished the death penalty.

Appeals. Nothing worked. This was Texas. Mercy for whom?
On death row Jackie sometimes asked his jailer for a cigarette.

On the campus of the University of Texas at Austin,
students marched in protest against the death penalty.
They chanted. They spoke over a microphone.
They carried signs. One student had once met Jackie.
She said his father had forbidden any more guns
in their house. Even so, his waning years were gloom.

Johnson Escalates a War

No school now in the mind's depths,
only the hedonism of daydreams.
And I roller-skate with ease
into a heavenly summer
in whose dog days I'd like to get some sun.
Even teachers kick back with beer.
I am seventeen in New Orleans
where the drinking age is eighteen. Who cares?
But tanning means anathema
to those as blond and fair-skinned as I am.
I don't tan, I stroke.
So my umbrella sticks in the sandy beach
like an American flag. I swim and wear
the sand up my feet like a sock. Today,
a shark reported in the lake's brackish water.
Last year a girl lost a foot to one.
It made the local news.
More the rare exception, however, than the rule.
Soon the lifeguards, too, will
head back to school. Soon the number of dead
from the distant war: on everyone's mind.

Language: French, Latin, German

I wanted to play werewolves, but the full moon was out.
Which scared me. An omen. I always felt sorry for Lon
Chaney, Jr. because he was helpless. His face showed it.
Besides, my family was moving. I felt like a zoo animal
changing cages. "Mom, let me be a seal doing its tricks."
I wasn't always in trouble with her. Sometimes I forgot
to take out the garbage. Then she started complaining.
Shook her fist. So I promised it wouldn't happen again.
Some of my friends broke into the local school. Destroyed
things. Then they had to go to court with their parents.
But Chris Sommers still let me shoot basketballs
into his backyard goal. A natural, he later played high school
basketball and baseball. His father coached him.
I played clarinet. Practicing seemed too much like a chore.
So I gave it up. What we're good at is where we go.
My tongue exercised. My tongue was my best friend.

Lunar

Reading a short story. Paging ahead to see how much
is left to read. Wow! I've come quite far! I must like it.
I must give my compliments to the author, via the editor.
The story is lyrical. Which helps me find something
to imitate. Now I learn the author's a poet. It says this:
a first publication. These animal images intrigue me.
Elephants being my favorite. Along with chimps and zebras.

Sunrise. How can I write about just one thing when
my mind is filled with so many? How can artists
even sleep when there is so much to be done? I can't.
Or maybe barely. I recall a trip to the New York World's Fair.
1965. Most impressed with the car James Bond drove
in *Goldfinger*. Also, the time capsule, sunk in the ground,
whose contents best represented America at that time.
The trip took three days by car from New Orleans.
My friend who owned the car even let me drive, and I
was barely sixteen, having just gotten my license.
A Burma Shave sign: "Ma loved Pa. Pa loved women.
Ma caught Pa with three gals a-swimmin. Here lies Pa."
Looking back, even a sixteen-year-old could laugh at that.

After our return, we washed the car with a garden hose
and buckets of soapy water. The day moon seemed not to move.
It took its time like the sun. The magic word was "space travel".
The astronauts were practicing. Getting ready for history.

Me and One I Imagine

I want to use words as often as comics get
their laughs from the crowd, their performance a poem.
They make a long time seem like a short time.
They make the laughter of everyone seem easier.
What's at stake? Art that appears to be effortless.
Moreover, don't doubt even humor from a poet.
Humor is as sought after as melody. O yes!

O yes, the sun is vanishing. Something not noticed
by the man living out his life beneath an overpass.
He thinks: beer. He thinks: where did my fate go wrong?
He thinks: pity me; what car passes not generous enough?
His sole pleasures: seeing Venus in the evening sky.
Talking at length to his peers, also at odds with the world.
If only he could sleep. If only the cold went elsewhere.
Today a woman passed him a hamburger from her window.
Sixty-eight now, he once got a medical discharge
from the Army after he reported hearing voices.
His family (a wife, two grown boys) left him because
of his violent behavior that got worse with alcohol.
He considers himself better off alone. He fears death.
Has mortified his flesh. "Perhaps if I could start
this life again," he wonders. Someday, he intuits,
he'll have to tell his few friends: until another time.

Missing My German

If only there were a bar nearby where I could
speak just German for entire evenings.
Whoever wants to keep up with their piano technique
can find a piano anywhere in the world. But using
Zoom is not like being within the physical presence
of another. I need to be able to look in someone's eyes.
Real eyes. For one has even much language thereby.

My German novel with the dog-eared page for my place.
Its author died four years ago, recognized in Germany.
I never had the pleasure of meeting Wilhelm Genazino.
He won what we know as the Pulitzer and National Book
Award among many others. They who rejected my
translation say he's too "weighty."
Meaning he's a thinker, a true poet.
He does so much more than tell an easy story.
Only seventy-five. His photos show him to be overweight.
Did he have diabetes? Heart trouble? Maybe a stroke?

I lost the friendship of another German I translated.
Tried to get in touch again. A few years went by.
I should have worked harder to be a friend.
What god has intervened to keep us apart? Regrets.

Ah well, Fontenot, it's not so bad. Think about your own
important work. Think about all else that matters.

Money, Gratis

I was wondering what ever happened to the public drinking fountains of my youth—they have become almost extinct—when a sparrow told me with its chirp that it was time to write again. This fleet-of-wing was bathing in the dust; consequently, its chirps grew louder and more frequent. What fun! What envy I felt for its joy! When was the last time I myself was so happy? Maybe a week ago. I found a one-hundred-dollar bill lying on the sidewalk. Like a small island. Lucky me. The bill proved essential for the many days I treated myself to coffee at my favorite coffee shop. But yes, you're tempted to spend it all at once, eating at a fine restaurant, the baked fish's eye staring at you, as if you did something wrong.

My Friend and I

We attended the Albert Einstein School
of Architecture, flunking out because we said
there were too many starry skyscrapers already.
My friend since childhood then went to sea.
He lassoed whales in his dreams, comfy
and pampered aboard an icebreaker. Whose freezer
broke and left everyone, unhappily without ice cubes.
How he ever got into the Coast Guard, no one knows.
He had flat feet, but I guess they were desperate
for people to work in the Arctic Ocean. Who would?
Icebreakers have a slanted bow to land atop the ice
and then use their weight to crack open a path. Wow!

Come to think of it, my ice cube maker makes a noise.
Since I rent, I'll contact the apartment manager.
Noise which keeps me awake! It started last week
before my party. Wall-to-wall people. So many of them
that I got trapped in a corner next to my toolbox.
I removed my chisel and hammer and banged out
a small hole in the wall I could escape through. Luckily
I had a sister nearby. In whose guest bed I could sleep!

Naming and Other Entrances

Our balance in existence. Not too withdrawn.
Not too overbearing. To lie in the middle ground.

So the leaves go on breathing in silence. And they take
lasting vacations in November. Good for them! For they
will return in spring, different and whole. Like the moon.
Going from emptiness to become its complete self.

Therefore, I must watch and listen as a receiver, alert.
One can't sleep one's way into or out of a poem.
Dreams yield only pieces, without being theory.
I see how chickens like to be around one another.
I see how there must be fewer leaves on the earth
than there are things in the universe. Listen. The cicadas
seem to utter their vivas. Roosters crow into habits.

But naming. I have to know the names to interact
more easily with others. What do you call the platform
on which icons are stored? A desktop? Thanks
for your help. One more word. To make a difference with.

New Day

I say, "poems like coffee shops, are meeting places, where
what happened yesterday can happen anew." The dog
is now content with his meal. The son shoots basketballs.
The incomplete moon sails safe as any navigator.
War in the Ukraine seems strange. The insanity of empire!
Nothing stops traffic from passing. Clouds rumble.
There are secrets between lines that no one will know.
How much to reveal? Best to mention wonder, amazement.
I am always open to greet them. More cannot be said.
It's Mardi Gras time in this city of my birth. I wish
I were a kid again when all appeared newer than now.
My parents took me to parades, dressed in a costume.
I liked the marching bands best, their sense of energy.
Music: sound organized. The tempo of drums. Heartbeats.

Red lights are so serious, rainy streets like mirrors at night.
Where have the dead gone? Why is it always time to begin
again? Nocturnal, rainy streets reflect the color of light.
I've already said that, but this is poetry. This is almost
the start of a new day. Everyone swims up from dreams.

Not Just a Thought

I make poems a habit as simply as some do
with crossword puzzles. The more you work,
the better you become. Remember the solution
to "slave": "esne". And that's just the beginning.

Is it better to go fast on a bicycle? Better
to live well than to spend time creating?
But there's life enough for both, you skeptics.

Today, for example, I walked my dogs, a notebook
in my pocket. Then jotted down a sentence.
The way Stevens did on his walk to the office.
The way Rilke did, leaving his stay at a hotel.

Sometimes the poem is not a creation, but a discovery.
Sometimes it's not just a thought, but an epiphany.

O Friend

De Tocqueville could be perceptive about America
in 1840 since one from abroad sees our country so well,
we being people who take much life for granted.
Thus, I could find Korea and Germany very revealing,
as a non-native. Had I remained longer in each,
I could have had certain insights like de Tocqueville.

Instead I must be content to glean from my own country.
It still suits me, my investment having been a lifetime.
It still lets me call a friend, enjoy a meal, sleep well.
O sleep, a night off from the job of being. O meals,
filling stations where the like-minded gather to give thanks.
O friend, constant as gravity, prepared as a lifeguard.

Once at a Zoo in England

My good deed for the bookstore—reshelving a book
of poems someone left in History—makes me suspect
a lapse in human behavior. Does someone want it hidden?
Only because no one might buy it in the wrong place?
Thus enabling one to have the book totally to oneself?
Another lapse: fifty-five years ago my genetics prof
left for his students journal articles in the reserve room.
Lo! When I got there, they had been razored out.
I did not yell "Help". I felt the mildest sense of loss
I had ever felt. Luckily our professor then decided
to assign what he mimeographed and passed out to all.
Which is why I dabbled in Buddhism. Welcome even the thief.

Welcome friends who arrive to drink wine—they called
beforehand. Put on a good face or nicely tell them how
out of sorts I feel in fact? There may be the coronavirus.
(Though each is over seventy, having already gotten the shots.)
But at least we're not in a combat zone like some.

At least my terrier is glad to see everyone sipping.
And it shows. The way joy shows for kids on their birthdays.
The way chimps smile at the zoo. What clowns, the chimps!

Once at a zoo in England, a man dressed up as if he were
a parking attendant. For twenty years he collected parking fees.
He was formal, yet amiable. No one ever questioned
his authority. Somehow. And he retired handsomely in Brazil.

Professor

Sam's being was stocked with friendship and steel nerves.
Who hasn't known others like him? Smiles and laughter
were their nutrients. They stopped smoking, the dangers clear.
Their partners always said the right things. Sam listened
more than those who could rattle on like fools.

And he got by with gardens. Trusted brief everlastings. Was
astonished by hummingbirds. Wanted to possess nothing.
Found clean grace in the way earthworms lived.
Whatever pain he bore, he forgot. Even the sun: a solace.

Quotidian

The self doesn't have a problem. The self is
the problem. So I exert it, then pamper it.
Which usually works. Exercise helps, and other people.
But one must find one's own way past the cop.
One must even come to terms with the uncertain.
Needed: a pet? a partner? a playground? a poet?
These thoughts make me think of how much I admire
mountain climbers and aviators. They are part
of those who seek out an adventure as a means of
completing what the body wants. What one dreams.
And me? A little wine helps. A bit of great music.
Beethoven, for example. The first composer to call
himself an artist. In the beginning Mozart and Haydn
ate with the servants. They were only craftsmen
who provided a commodity. Now great musicians
inspire the same awe as others in show business.
Yet naming someone a famous poet is an oxymoron.
They exist without fanfare. So the cows return
in their slow way. So I find work, idle on the page.

Rebuttal

Whoever frames a soul within the body—creates art.
Whoever finds a spirit in the sun—is already wise.

Therefore, make the most of sunshine, the most of what
Apollo can do. Call to the blackbirds as they
fly away from a tree in the shape of a tree.
Some noise has scared them. They reconvene elsewhere.

I, too, settle down elsewhere. At a café? At a bar?
Any place I can leave my TV for. To talk. To sip wine.
One café I go to plays only classical music.
The local station with no commercials, instead fund drives
three times a year. No DJ, solipsistic. Rather, a noble voice.
In a time that celebrates noise, here is a rebuttal,
praising the wish for something smart, something sensible.

Seed Time

What a surprise to notice my blue veins as rivers
with their tributaries! Maps I love as much as seeing
geese in flight. Their journey calls our own to mind.
Their journey must inspire us to circumnavigate the earth.
Every so often pilots try to set another record.

I myself once flew a plane. But never in a war.
It was a way to gain the focus of a bird.
A way to feel as if more than the ground was home.
I even took my friends on flights. They seemed
secure and rapt for the experience. Clouds came
and went. The engine hummed; a spinning prop.

A lack of money made me look for something else.
The sun rose and the light shone on my paper
filling up with parts of speech and end-stopped lines.
I read and read. Here finally was the means
to spend what time I'd give to launch a self.
Seed time. One of gestation. Then a bringing forth.

Simply Pinholes

Not enough times have I listened to the silence
of stars. A lack in me, something missing, kept me
dumb, though their light is reminder now.
And speaks more truth than any judge, anywhere.
For it settles nice and easy into pinholes, happy
to be pinholes and not just some loose change.
Meanwhile, flowers stay in pots, not a single thought
among them. That way I get on with the day.

It's dawn. I am moved by the reddening blotch
at the bottom of the sky. Birds change songs into spring.
Then whooshes of cars. A boy on a bike. The creek talks.
A sense of rain. The clouds, their blackness, say so.
Last night the weatherman already predicted change.
Last night there was already wind. In a mad March.

Part Three
The Forests of Autumn

Sisters

My ken of things is limited. Kant said it would be.
Luckily, I don't need to know everything to lead my life.
I can hardly picture Kleist's struggle with Kant.
How our senses are not reliable, how what we
believe is truth only seems to be, and how in life
after death no truth can help us perfect ourselves.
Neurasthenic anyway, Kleist staggered in spirit.

Both of us: close to our sisters, but Kleist lacked
a sense for money and depended on Ulrike often.
Sheila won't go that far, yet escaping
to Panama City Beach from Hurricane Ida,
she bought my meals, my beer, my place
to stay. What generosity! What luck! Imagine that.

Sixties Blues

Always I was headed in another direction
from the cricket chirping inside a padlock
while trying to put my gym clothes in a locker.
In Phys. Ed. Harry Larsen played first base, but he
threw the ball so hard that, even with my glove
as protection, the middle finger broke
at the topmost joint. He was my best friend
through grade school, junior high, and high school.
He fought in Vietnam, then became a social worker.
I myself wanted to know how Tristan Tzara could
write such beautifully complex poems, me being
only eighteen but already cornered by a Muse,
walking down Royal Street on Mardi Gras's big day.
My innocence was put in prison when JFK died.
I tried to deliver a speech, for president, as he might have.
The applause of the student body, in a hot auditorium,
gave me a new direction, even though I was scared
at the mike. Now I would give the poem a fighting chance.
Now I would start to read Waley's lovely translations.

In my pockets was a dream only I could make sense of.
I seemed to be swimming in the lake of my own mind.
Sharks made their way into brackish water, and one girl
was bitten, and the world was still uneasily happy.
"Jump in the lake," the moon whispered. "Get into
the swing of things," my mother kept telling me.
Why does one never unlearn how in fact to swim?
I, provided I'm not drowning, am happy in water.

Anger is fine since I always learn much from it.
Be compliant, that's my motto. Enjoy your meal!
Try to be nice to the cop who has dutifully pulled you over.
Read Robert Walser. He answers cosmic questions.
And my mother said repeatedly, "Cut your hair, cut
the grass." She must have had something against growth.

Special Place

When I put my first "When" on the poem, I think of
a composer inking in his first note, a quarter note
for a clarinet that will open the piece, a short
concerto in which a piano does most of the work.
I take stock of my doubts as priests do with sinners.
I single out cats for their mysticism, eager pups
for their hedonism. Should I have hope for New Orleans
and a decent season? Losing quarterback Brees: ominous.
Losing the Kennedys as well as Dr. King made
my boyhood innocence seem like witnessing
the violence of fairy tales all over again. Good thing
we went to the moon. Good thing Nixon resigned.
I keep a special place in my spirit open to body.
I keep a special place in my spirit open to soul.

Spring 2

It's so early in spring inside the car that I have to wear
the memory of a jacket given to the Salvation Army.
My ingenuity is driving, headed for a vacation spot
of long ago: my childhood. I need to talk to my younger self.
If he's not there, I'll just have to imagine the whole thing.
He may have some information I no longer have.
Valuable as a diamond. More informative than TV.
He might be able to teach me to be grateful again.
He might be able to teach me the importance of pets.

Failing that, I'll ask the sea to give me a lecture.
No one will ever waste a lecture on me, still eager.
Already the moon hides itself inside a beehive.
Whose bees know the flowers better even than we do.
The sun only gives without ever taking, lasting as long
as we need to imagine. But the sun's not up for a promotion.
Having been happy all along about what it's doing.

Having been happy all along about what I'm doing,
I think the rain is as lovely as another cool morning.

T'ang Inspiration

The poets count on the fact that, of all possible things,
we have seen what they see or can imagine it.
But our minds might ask: huh? Their words could resist
our intelligence. Still the light. Still we hope for
an epiphany in which we hear ourselves say: wow.
Be patient, we rest assured, something will come of this.

Take the word "sun" for example: all inclusive in itself.
My sun is a painter, and it works by day. What
could be more apparent? I want to keep readers,
not turn them away. Which reminds me. This poem.
I will have to give it the limpidity of Tu Fu.

I read with only one eye open. Does it matter?
Machinery rattles in the courtyard where workmen
are redoing the inside of a swimming pool.
Money affects me, but in the T'ang Dynasty they always
worried about war. How difficult their lives had to be!
Yet they wrote of the beauty of wild geese as well.
I have stolen my love of the moon from them.
What did the talkative flower vendor care
if new laws from the government were posted?
And it may not be true: the story of a drunken Li Po
drowning. As he tried to embrace the moon. In a river.

Teachers On the Beach

How hard to write in coffee shops! My ears
prefer to eavesdrop. Only when there is so much
talk that I understand nothing can I write.
Now Miles Davis is seeping from the heavens. Hooray!
A wordless enchantment. A trumpet in love.

But suddenly I see myself in 1958, listening.
Chuck Willis. "What am I living for, if not for you?"
"Oh, oh, nobody else, nobody else will do." Top that,
I thought back then. Ah, what a simpleton I was.
I bought it the way most buy their lottery tickets.

So I'm careful what I buy these days. The women
on the bus build entire conversations around prices.
"Did you see that asparagus went up sky-high?"
And so forth. I'm more interested in feeling what
the waves might be saying. Those teachers
with their fingers to their lips: "Shhh..."

Text Message to the Gods

O laudable gods, I see all of you everywhere,
In the body of a squirrel hopping to bury another nut,
In the plight of zebras escaping from lions, also you.
So much do you try to please me with your images.
You have been here not less than many millennia.
Of a sudden, I am ready to forgive any fault of yours.
Just as I am ready to be kinder to myself. Especially
In view of your more tragic guises: floods, fires, wars.
Do we humans displease you if you're out of sorts?
Because of you I have studied much Goethe, Hoelderlin,
Nietzsche as well as the many people I often meet.
Something godly about all of them, the world being
Not always a demon from the abyss. Let me remember
You and your gifts should I gloom. Let me see you
As a fireman desperate to save any life he can.

The Congress Avenue Bridge

With my translated novel I feel like the hundred
singers at an audition—only one can be chosen
and I am among the sad, unlucky ones. Literature
has gotten to be as competitive as the world
of entertainment. It wasn't always this way.
Suddenly the former zeitgeist is now in eclipse.
Therefore, I write to please just myself
and maybe my friends who still remain loyal.

But let's not dwell on the self. Let's look at
the millions of bats. They burst from the Congress
Avenue bridge to ease their hunger for insects.
If only we could keep them as pets, close to us!
We envy their freedom. Their spontaneity. Like
racehorses coming out of the starting gate. Bravo!

The Earth, Running Out of Time

My mind, sometimes a stranger to the aims of words.
And I owe my allegiances not to a flag but to
A brotherhood and sisterhood of those like me
Who deal with song, as steadfast as some scientist.
As prone to call up notions all the prudent know.

So, I read widely. Who can ever trace my steps?
It's not important that I'm one without biography.
It's not important that the sun will outlive me.
My mind, sometimes a stranger to the aims of words.

Today I want to fashion verse. I want to sing in ways
That emphasize our lives and what's at stake in terms
Of loss. An old concept. Which calls for new imaginings.

The pigeon loses feathers, and we lose our hair.
The obvious is how we feel and thus lament.
Even the wind will work against us if it's strong.
Likewise, the water free to flood. And storms. What then?
Wildfires sweep the land of homes. A broom of flames.
Why is the news crew asking folks: what now?
It's pointless and demeaning, for we know
Already how they feel. Leave bad enough alone.

My mind, sometimes a stranger to the aims of words.
In nineteen sixty-five kids paddled down our street
You couldn't see. Had Betsy's waters risen higher,
We would have lost the things that kept us comfortable.
But luckily the gods spared us. Another chance. A light.

The Few That Get Away

Fish don't recognize our hooks.
They succumb like those in gulags.
The few that get away are strong enough
to pop the line and see another day below,
the hook still part of them—but not as
a reminder—unremembered; they bite again.

My fisherman father gave up on me
who couldn't stand to be a fish's jailer.
So he taught me how to give a car a tune-up.
But computers put an end to what I wanted
to learn. I now moved my hand across
a page. I built stanzas like fortresses.
The spark plugs of my being became metaphors.
Bodily organs, they kept me alive. And I sensed
a world with locks my keys could open.

The German Word for "Cook"

The last name "Koch" has always fascinated me.
The mayor of New York pronounced it: Kotch.
The New York School Kenneth pronounced it: Coke.
It's hard for Americans to make the German
sound "ch" aspirated in the uvula.
Whereas the Germans can't produce,
only naturally, the "th" sound in "this".
Instead, they'll say "zis". To pronounce
a foreign language may be difficult.
Which is why all of us can detect accents
in those who are not native speakers.
For the most part anyway. With exceptions.
Why do people talk at all? If not,
we'd be a whole heck of a lot worse.

The Homelessness of Fish

The daylight was wearing boxing gloves, so we shut
the curtains in order not to provoke the daylight.
We felt strangely happy rolling head over heels
like a wheel the day before Russia slapped the Ukraine.
Our dilemma: how to climb a mountain in summer attire.
Finally, we gave up on it. Finally, the sun set without haste.

Are olive green shirts in style these days? Are cars wishing
they were electric instead of making the weather unhappy?
We know. We watch the news. We get the Buddha involved.
Sitting meditation takes precedence over everything else.
Raising pigs almost takes precedence over everything else.
We could complain, but grackles complain enough
for all of us. And they sing dirges with the end of day.

If the cold rain is dreamed, will the mind get wet?
Be clever as a traffic light going from red to green.
Be cross with thunderstorms that won't let up.
Be amazed at the dolphins doing their easy tricks.

And never wholly forget the homelessness of fish.

The Questions

Today some trees are naked, others clothed. I think
about photosynthesis. I'd like to be oxygen exhaled
by leaves. For once I would even feel useful.
In all the world: the same. We can't hear trees breathing.
Unlike a long-distance runner after her race.

I wanted to be a sprinter on the school's track team.
But I washed out. Instead, I took photographs
for the newspaper. I had a hard time talking to others.
Clumsy years. Teachers liked me for my industry.
My compliance. No thoughts about the world. No thoughts
about America's place. My father fought a war that was
to end all wars. I had my family & a friendly mixed breed.
Didn't realize that others suffered for their inequality.
Clueless. I was clueless. The moon meant much to me.
I watched the lunar landing. Never slept in class.
I would not take my coffee black. Added cream & sugar.

Young, my brother tried to catch an idle bumblebee
by its wings. A great way to be stung. He didn't care.
He flunked out of college. Whenever he rode—at ten—
a bicycle, he'd sometimes not look where he
was going. A brain tumor removed him from view.

What do the years tell us? I'm receptive to any answer.
Still, it's enough. Enough just to love the questions.

Ken Fontenot

This Early

In my dream an old man drinking milk
from a baby bottle. He with the brain of a child.
Later, I got out of my car, and my house
was walking toward me like a relative.
Awake, I needed to fill up my gas tank.
The birds that day kept themselves hidden.
The day moon was a smile. I smiled back.

The stars are old enough to have my homage.
Even the sequoias I consider to be my friends.
Those monuments, sanctuaries, works of art.

Meanwhile, my memories wonder why your body
mutinied on you, why your visit to earth was so brief.
That is, now you might know of a better place.
This early, this early, old friend, in eternity.

Time to Come Inside

Does happiness enter or leave me? I'd like to praise
the starlight too as it finds a brief home in my eyes.
I welcome it which tells us an undeniable truth.
More we tyros can't say, but let the astrophysicists
sort it out. I await any new enlightenment from them.
I await the new day and what it carries all day long.
Pleasant surprises? Some luck? Small kindnesses? Souls
that are beautiful? Animals and children easy to love?

But so badly did I want independence that I sold all
my books for practically nothing. I needed to enter
each of them from the front and leave by the back.

And I still have feelings for broken chairs. Not their
fault. It's those kids. Neighbors. They play too hard.
They open their mouths and breathe out stars.
Their dog jumps in and wears water. Then mothers
summon them in even earlier than the day before.
There's no real message in this. Only parenting.

Tiny Comet

Today I want to count—the number of dashes
in Dickinson's poetry. To get an idea of her silences.
No one could ever use them—the way she did. That
would be fatal. So I stay content with my own few—
knowing that much of syntax depends on them.

I stay content with clouds motionless—moving almost
imperceptibly. Rain on the way—faceless, insistent rain.
More good than harm—even if it brings strong winds.
What could the gray clouds be telling us, friends
of the earth that now needs more help than ever?
Do they tell us to recall the water cycle we learn
in school? Do they give us hope we'll never go thirsty?

I have a tiny comet in my ear! Roaring to come out
and spread my world with its cometic presence. Bravo!
Let the earth go on, with vigor. Let the seas shine.
Let telescopes far out in space tell everyone about
how much light lives in the universe beside dark.

To Have a Sense for Animals

The engine whine of a motorcycle picking up speed.
Chopin on my CD player. His brilliant, sui generis waltzes.
Of which melody is a part. I'm in such a mood as
to believe how my room's light can make all the difference.
Outside are cirrus clouds, high, well out of reach.
It's February, an incredibly mild day, while in Boston
there's a paralyzing nor'easter with its snow dumping
nearly house-high, if it were never cleared away.
I feel a determined door as it opens into the past.
I feel a sense of where the mind is supposed to be.

But who admires the whales as much as I do? Who
else loves the seals in their performance for
which they've been trained? Then the treat of a fish.
B. F. Skinner argued like a judge that we, too,
are conditioned. Even though some may have doubts.

I'd like to learn what the chimps say to each other
with their voices and gestures. In fact, a scientist has
already done so. The dense forests are theirs.
And they live as mankind lives, in their own competitive
societies. Let's like them as forerunners, as teachers.
While Jane Goodall has been saintly in her devotion.

The Forests of Autumn

Homage to Robert Walser (1878-1956)

Despite all the laptops no one can take
their eyes from, despite all the phones people
pass their time with, the book is still my god.
In the coffee shop I read the essays of Coetzee,
a Nobel Prize winner. I'm interested in Walser
especially. With his ill soul, he spent his last
twenty-seven years in madhouses. I empathize,
my own mental health as fragile as his was.
Both of us nearly unable to hold onto jobs.
Luckily, as a Swiss citizen, he couldn't
live on the street, his fate in today's world.

But in my seventy-fifth year my soul has improved.
I still lament the deaths of drug users everywhere.
Life is something they've never bought tickets to.
Yet insanity can be innocent. The man who walks
through the coffee shop every day can't sit down.
Notice the swarm of bees buzzing wild inside him.
He looks around. Stands still. Then keeps walking.
Walser, too, liked to hike. Which might have saved
him from a heart attack until he was seventy-eight.
Which was his passport into the forests of autumn.

Werner Drive

The dog had a blue bark. He was part of a pack
of strays that wandered down my boyhood street.
I rode my bike and he chased me, trying to bite
my moving foot. I kicked, which drove him off.
And I still don't know what prompts a dog
to chase a car. Doggy psychology must surely exist.

My street was built over a pig farm. First blacktop.
Then a few years later concrete. I recall the huge trucks.
How the back spun around to keep the cement wet.
At the amusement park we kids, too, spun around
on a ride in which the floor dropped down, only
to leave us stuck to the sides by centrifugal force.
What a wonder to be like an astronaut and defy gravity!

In 1965 (Hurricane Betsy) Werner Drive became a river.
Kids paddled in skiffs up and down a street
you couldn't see. The water rose just below
the doorsill. Whew! Nothing given to the flood.
But forty years later—exactly—Katrina left us
water house-high. Good thing my sister had
evacuated. Good thing I lived in Austin then.
For all my manuscripts would have floated away
with family photos and everything else so many
understood in the new thinking, and the old: loss.

Ken Fontenot

What I Still Feel

Beer companies make money because everyone
thinks they'll have just one more beer.
Now that I've taken psychoactive medication
for forty-five years, alcohol no longer affects me.
But maybe that's a good thing: I save money.

Here I've had nothing to say to this poem for weeks.
Today I had a thought. Though one not worthy enough.
So I'll patiently wait. Rilke said patience is everything.
He, probably more read in America than in Germany now.

Does anyone ask oneself, "What's Ken up to at the moment?"
Does anyone believe one knows more than anyone else?

I'm no polymath. I practice my German. Brush my teeth.
Take a long time to leave my chair to brush my teeth.
Better to spend days on walks. I see trees Hurricane Ida
uprooted. I'm like Frank O'Hara. I did this. I did that.

As a boy I aimed my BB gun at the full moon
and pulled the trigger. I climbed trees with other
kids and once fell out, breaking my arm. A cast.
They put my forearm in a cast. Other kids signed
their names on it in ink. Many of them laughed at me.
That's just what kids do. Another time Billy Bean
punched me in the stomach. A sucker punch.
Sometimes—I never know when—I still feel it.

What Money Is Like

You're just like your stars, pleasant and balmy.
But why do you keep dreams in your pockets?
Why does the day pick itself up and continue?
I sense your mind feeling its way around
in cerebral darkness. And this changes everything.
No longer do you keep hiding yourself in words.
No longer do you stop me from getting wet in rain.
All recalls a sad happiness, an easy way out. Survive!

I would like to go fast on my bicycle that thieves must
be thinking of stealing. Ubiquitous, they need to change
their lives even though complacency is beginning to set in.
They're in a rut like the rest of us, happy for risks.
They seem to be under the spell of fallen angels.

I'm growing used to becoming old without guarantees.
I buy you a coffee and feel my money slipping away.
But I'm no miser. Get over it, scrooge. Think about
how far your next paycheck will go, saving a bit of it.
Money is like the flowing of blood: it keeps moving.

What Spirit

I would say Chopin is the more Apollonian,
and Schumann the more Dionysian. Listening
to Chopin's mazurkas, I think: how stately.
Schumann shows me the world to be dreamland.
Both great enough to imagine giving them as gifts.
Tho Chopin disliked Schumann's music, each dedicated
a piece to the other. Schumann's sad fate: madness.
And Chopin declined after leaving George Sand.

Each brings joy to me, as if they equaled great sunsets.
Tonight, in fact, I missed the stars, so important
was pen wedded to paper. Surprise grew in me.
As well as the feeling the mind was its own reward.
But who needs to be called Romantic in a time of
worldwide illness? Apropos is Rothko's "Black on Maroon"
(1958). His tones are somber, even solemn.
Best to think about sending modest contributions
to those most in need. Yet who are everywhere.
If charity begins at home, I don't want to be home.
I want to assess, then act. My pets can help.
They, like refugees, are irreplaceable. Remember both.
Remember with what spirit the farmer treats his crops.

The Forests of Autumn

What Was I Thinking?

A public shaming unsettles me—the one in Hawthorne's
Scarlet Letter, for example. The policing of morals
made public. Adulterers are brought to the town scaffold.
Likewise, in my novel *For Mr. Raindrinker*, a Creole
of color elementary teacher lectures a black pupil
for stealing, in front of the entire fourth grade class.
I should have had the teacher resolve this in private.
Could the shaming have happened in a real classroom?
Possibly. What was I thinking? Writers must think hard.

Mistakes. Worse than doing a math problem wrong?
Of course. I have, as a child, lost my father's tools.
I have once run a stop sign, hitting another car.
I have worn soiled underpants in the hospital to
my mother's embarrassment. I have failed exams.
I have acted like a thief. Have broken grumpy Smith's
window, batting a baseball. Have sneezed once
into a friend's box of cocaine which flew everywhere.
And some of these things are—what?—laughable.

Ken Fontenot

With Dancing in Mind

I never entered the heated room
of agonistic literary life. Instead I followed
shadows falling across doors
as they opened. They were like dreams ending.
The crickets sang. Later the moon resembled
an eye without iris or pupil
as if a doctor shone a light into it.
I wished for a chance, a broom to sweep
everything clean. But two gods descended,
two little gods: a dog and a cat.
Somewhere a necessary disquiet played a fiddle.
People danced all night into each other's desires.
Let me have this night, I thought,
this night to set all remaining nights afloat.

Years Before His Insanity

Clara Schumann had a French accent, speaking
German! It hardly mattered, she being a virtuoso
of the piano, known throughout Europe. Still,
she had to compete with Robert for time on the piano.
Their only one. With a family of needy children,
they couldn't even begin to afford having
a second. So she worried about lapsing,
giving in to his moods that made him difficult.
Compose? Yes, her father taught her to, early on.
She herself believed a woman shouldn't
equal her husband. But how could she be
a mother, a concert pianist, *and* a great composer?
She needed Nietzsche's later concept of self-esteem.
She needed to have another two centuries on her side.

Acknowledgements

"Glory Be" and "What Spirit" appeared in *Christianity and Literature*

"If Only" appeared in *Borderlands*

"Invocation of Angels" appeared in the Houston *Chronicle*, and the San Antonio *Express-News*

About Ken Fontenot

Ken Fontenot received an MA in German language and literature from the University of Texas at Austin (with a thesis on Heinrich von Kleist) and studied in Freiburg, Germany under a DAAD fellowship during the school year of 1986-87. His early book of poems, *All My Animals and Stars* (1988), won the Austin Book Award, and his poetry collection *In a Kingdom of Birds* won the 2012 Texas Institute of Letters award for best poetry book in Texas. In 2015 a fourth book of poems, *Just a Trace of Moon*, appeared from Pinyon Publishing. His manuscript Collected Translations from the German and his translation of a novel by Wilhelm Genazino have recently been completed. His novel is *For Mr. Raindrinker*, published in 2015 by Alamo Bay Press. He writes: "I believe the poet has the right to use his entire life as material for his work. The past is never off-limits. Too, poems can be imaginary. Poets should have the same license as novelists. How dull autobiography alone can sometimes be!" Fontenot's book of poetry titled *To Those Born Later* was released by Alamo Bay Press in 2022.

About Octavio Quintanilla

Cover artist **Octavio Quintanilla** is the 2025 Texas Poet Laureate and is the author of the poetry collections *If I Go Missing*, *The Book of Wounded Sparrows*, which was longlisted for the National Book Award, and *Las Horas Imposibles / The Impossible Hours*, winner of the 2024 Ambroggio Prize of the Academy of American Poets. Octavio is the founder and director of the literature & arts festival, VersoFrontera, publisher of Alabrava Press. He has a PhD from the University of North Texas, and teaches Literature and Creative Writing at Our Lady of the Lake University. He was recently inducted into the Texas Institute of Letters.

Recent Books from

ALAMO BAY PRESS

Forty Years at Paisano: A Literary History
by Audrey Slate

Answers Without Questions: Conversations about Writing and Creativity
by Lowell Mick White

Broken to Mend: Poems
by Ricardo Tane Ward-Ramirez

Mi Tía Cajeta: A Story in Spanish and English
by Nancy Perez Fugere

For more information, contact Alamo Bay Press

www.alamobaypress.com

Praise for Ken Fontenot

Ken Fontenot's *The Forests of Autumn* celebrates a life lived in poetry. Exploring his Cajun heritage, his struggles with existential angst, as well as his love of classical music, philosophy, the German language, and other writers, Fontenot's poems are "not so much a creation as a discovery." A true original who likes "to be me often rather than sometimes," Fontenot "empoem(s)" us with tenderness, wit, and the mystery of the everyday.
   —Grace Bauer, author of *Unholy Heart: New & Selected Poems*

Poems bestow kinds of knowledge other modes of expression often can't. Ken Fontenot knows this. "Forget fame, Fontenot," he tells himself. To us he says, "Unlike Apollinaire, I don't ask you to take pity on me," because, as he admits, "I took a chance at being a poet with no certainty." But now, thinking of boyhood friends, those "swallowed up" both by and from his neighborhood New Orleans streets, he laments that he alone is "left to empoem you." Which makes him pose the knowledge question: "What do we gather growing older?" Maybe, he surmises, to become the "one who observes everything"? That's an admirable Taoist aspiration, but what knowledge, really, is thus "gathered"? Personally, I revere his mixed-faith response, given, as usual, in his own "Cajun idiolect": "I need to enter a broom's straw while I perceive / the mop's faith."
   —Kurt Heinzelman, author of *Pollen, Salt, & Chimes: New Poems & Select Others*

I always look forward to a new book by Ken Fontenot. He reminds me of Chinese poets I admire like Du Fu—wise, charming, educated and playful. The Forests of Autumn—I love that title—continues and expands upon themes we've seen in his previous collections: classical music, childhood memories, families, German philosophers, and nature, especially birds. Over a distinguished career spanning several decades, he has honored his talents. Readers are rewarded on every page.
   —Richard Cole, author of *Song of the Middle Manager*

www.ingramcontent.com/pod-product-compliance
Lightning Source LLC
Chambersburg PA
CBHW060537080526
44586CB00012B/773